Published by Mind Body Spirit Direct 2004

ISBN 0-9547036-0-X

Printed by Biddles Ltd

Mind Body Spirit Direct Ltd, 755 Fulham Road, London SW6 5UU
Tel: 020 7731 2828

E-mail: info@mindbodyspiritdirect.co.uk

Contents

Books by the same author include:

The Meditation Plan, Piatkus Books

Realise Your Inner Potential (co-authored with George King), Aetherius Press

The Magic of Healing, Thorsons

Unlock Your Psychic Powers, St. Martin's Press

Little Book of Karma, Thorsons

Little Book of Yin and Yang, Thorsons

Website: www.richardlawrence.co.uk

Bestselling author Richard Lawrence is often described as one of Britain's leading experts on Mind, Body and Spirit. He frequently writes for major newspapers and magazines, and appears on TV and radio around the world. He is European Secretary of The Aetherius Society and a Director of the Inner Potential Centre in London.

Acknowledgements

I am deeply grateful to all those who assisted me in making this book possible, particularly to John Holder, Mel Donovan, Steve Gibson, Alice Dyson, Nikki Perrott, Noemi Perkin and Mark Bennett for their invaluable help.

Foreword

There was a legend told in ancient India. One day the king of the gods, Indra, decided to inhabit the body of a pig to see what it was like. It did not take him long to get used to it - he forgot all about his life as a god and became thoroughly contented in his new existence. His fellow gods were distraught and tried to reason with him, but Indra told them that he had a lovely sow and piglets and a very comfortable sty - everything, in fact, that any self-respecting pig could desire. There was no reason to look further. Drastic action was the only solution. The gods cut open the pig body and released the god within, back to his former glory and a true knowledge of what he really was.

Richard Lawrence's methods are a little gentler than this, but their aim is the same - to help you break through the restrictions of self-imposed conditioning and discover, not so much a new world of experience, as a very old world of *being* that has always been there, but which we have subconsciously chosen to forget.

I first met Richard in the mid-70s, when he was a young man determined to discover the spiritual truths behind life. While many people in the first flush of youth lose their ideals and determination, and the inspiration that makes them believe that they can do anything they determine, I can safely say, having known Richard as a good friend ever since, that he has never wavered in that determination. Today he is one of the finest teachers of the mental and spiritual sciences anywhere in the world. He has inspiration and flair, is unmotivated by money and has that vital ability in a teacher - the ability to communicate his vision and inspiration to others. This quality comes shining through these pages: his is a voice of someone who is not concerned with theory or high-flown ideas, but of someone who has a really profound knowledge of his subject and can convey it simply and concisely.

I detect another voice here - it is the voice of his teacher, the great western Yogi who Richard worked with for over 25 years, Dr. George King. He believed that if you really know what you are talking about, you can teach in a way that is direct, effective and, above all, safe for the practitioner. It is a form of teaching in which the yogi keeps the greater portion of their vast knowledge hidden, only giving the student that which will really benefit them. You might not guess it when you read this book, but the exercises you are about to be introduced to are the product of a mind that knows far more than is revealed here, and which has had many great experiences through performing exercises just like these. It is a work by someone who knows what he is talking about.

Richard was one of the leading lights behind the founding of the Inner Potential Centre in London in 1999. The Complete Workout for the

Mind described in Part One of this book is not just something to be read. It has, to accompany it, a DVD, CD and cassette tape. It is also the basis for lectures and workshops run by The Inner Potential Centre in the UK and elsewhere. So, if you feel that you want to move beyond the realm of words into guided instruction, you will be well provided for by contacting us as detailed in the Appendix.

The beautiful exercises in this book are absolute gems, which really will work with the minimum of practice. Together they form a complete system that you can use throughout your life. Richard is too modest to make this claim, so I will make it for him - these exercises, if practised diligently every day, will undoubtedly lead you into the greater mystic states. But that is beyond the main objective of this book. It is designed for the person who wants to find a way to move beyond the restrictions of everyday life and discover the world within - a world of excitement, stimulation and adventure. A world that can manifest in the mind, even though your physical circumstances remain unchanged. A world in which we find our reason for living and the way to make it happen. It is a simple objective, but one which is within the capacity of all of us. If it is your aim in life, then this wonderful little book will - not might, but *will* - help you on your way.

- Steve Gibson

Steve is a Director of The Inner Potential Centre. He is also an expert on the mind and an experienced teacher of spiritual practices. He runs a group of public companies specialising in creativity and new technology.

meditation

Meditation is a most wonderful practice – everyone can do it, and it can transform your life. It is one of the simplest things in the world, but not always the easiest: it means watching and controlling the mind, which most people very rarely do. When you start to meditate, you begin to find a deep peace, to get a clearer perspective on life and learn to cope better with all kinds of things that you may have found stressful before. The ancient practitioners of yoga – and I am not referring so much to the physical exercises of *hatha* yoga (beneficial though they are) as to the deep mystic forms of yoga, such as *raja* and *jnani* yoga – used meditation as a path to enlightenment. In ancient India the earliest masters of yoga, known as the *rishis,* said that by watching the mind you prove that you are more than the mind, otherwise you could not watch it. They taught that you are actually a divine soul and that you have a higher self, which can be contacted through meditation.

Meditation can take you all the way to enlightenment, as detailed in Part Two of this book, which is entitled: A Discovery of the Spirit. Most people are unwilling to take it that far, but everyone can still enhance their life enormously by practising meditation in a more basic form. This will be the focus of Part One, entitled: A Complete Workout for the Mind.

Part I

a complete workout for the mind

~

introduction

Meditation is something which takes getting used to. We are programmed in life, particularly by our educational system, to use our mind in a certain way. A piece of equipment called an electroencephalograph is used by scientists to measure the rate of brain waves, and it has been shown that when we start to meditate, the rate of these brain waves starts to slow down. When we are in our normal waking state, probably the state you are in right now as you are reading this book, or when you are making a phone call, cooking a meal or driving a car, we are in the Beta state. That signifies a brainwave rate of between 13 and 28 per second voltage. As you start to enter meditation, you move into the next category, Alpha, which is ten per second. Then, if you take it even further and you enter a deeper mystical condition, you are moving into Theta, which is perhaps between three and six per second. And finally there is Delta, which is associated with deep sleep and is below three per second.

Most people, who don't meditate or do any other kind of spiritual exercises, spend their lives in either Beta or Delta. Throughout the day they are in Beta and at night in Delta. People seem to have completely lost the art of relaxation. The average person's idea of relaxation might be going to a football match, clubbing, or watching an exciting film, but, fun though these things may be, they do not truly relax the mind. Such a person operates in Beta all day, goes to sleep at night and enters Delta, until the alarm goes off and they are thrust back into Beta, and so it goes on. The stages in between Beta and Delta are entirely missed out, all the experience that can be gained from the mind in these states of consciousness are lost to them. Meditation will take you into those areas. Some of the benefits which have been claimed for meditation, and specifically the Alpha state, have included clearing up psychosomatic ailments, reducing the risk of stress-related illness, lowering blood pressure, and slowing down the aging process. There is no doubt that meditation can transform your life.

I was taught by Dr George King (1919-1997) who was a genuine master of yoga. He was a wonderful teacher who taught me the basics of self-development: concentration and contemplation. He said that the highest state of meditation was something very rarely attained on Earth, the state described in Sanskrit as *samadhi*. This deep state of consciousness, which he could attain, involves the heartbeat actually stopping and really deeply elevated conditions being brought about in which you are able to completely *know* – in the fullest sense of the word – whatever it is that you choose to meditate on. For most of us this is quite a long way down the road, but you can start at a much more basic level and still get great results.

I focus on three stages of meditation in this workout: imagination, intuition and inspiration. Exercising these three under-used aspects of the mind is key to finding true success, happiness and fulfilment. The brain is not the fountain of all our knowledge, nor is it the essence of our being, or even of our personality. It is like a radio receiver set, and the thoughts that come through the brain are like radio waves. Just as you can tune the frequency of a radio, so can you tune the frequency of your brain. You have the potential to control your own mind more than you ever dreamt possible.

you are
not the
slave
of your
mind

Getting Started

So many people, when they wake up in the morning feeling depressed, annoyed or some other negative emotion, think that it is out of their control. "Oh, I'm in a bad mood today and there's nothing I can do about it" is the general attitude. But when you become a meditator, you start to realise that you can choose, you can start to control your own moods, you are not the slave of your mind. In this workout, try to look at your mind in that way, look upon your brain as a receiver set for the thoughts and the feelings that flow through it. This is the beginning of "watchfulness", or as the Buddhists call it "mindfulness". Allow – and that is a key word in all spiritual development – *allow* thoughts to come to you. You will probably be shocked, or at the very least a little surprised, by some of the thoughts that do come to you. But don't let that stop you – allow your brain to receive them, and then let them flow through you. Rather like radio waves, thoughts pulse, they move in wave motion. As you watch them they will come and go, and come and go – allow them to do that. Don't get wrapped up in them, don't start focusing on any of them, don't try to start to work anything out. Just let them come and go. You are now the observer, slowly realising that you are more than your mind.

0.1 The Sitting Position

Keeping the spine straight: The first thing you need to do with meditation is to be seated in the correct position. Some people will know a posture, also called an asana, such as *padma* (Sanskrit for "lotus"), which they can adopt if they so choose, but this is not necessary. You can do all the exercises in this book seated on a hard-backed wooden chair. Make sure your spine is straight, but at the same time try to keep the body as relaxed as possible. Place the palms facing downwards on the knees with the fingers slightly out-stretched and rest the head back a little on the neck. If you find that there is tension in your shoulders, as you probably will after a busy day, you can loosen them up by rolling them around a bit. When you have done this try to become completely still. Ideally your body should be as physically clean as possible when you meditate, and you should also wear clean clothes – preferably ones you don't normally wear when you go out.

0.2 The Technique of Deep Breathing

The deeper you breathe, the deeper you perceive: According to the yogis of old, the science of breathing is the secret of living. There are two reasons for this: the first is the one that we all know – that by breathing we inhale oxygen which is, quite literally, vital to our physical well-being. The second reason, which is just as important if not more so, is that when we breathe we draw a certain type of energy into ourselves. This energy has been known by many names: in China it is known as *qi* (also spelt "*ch'i*"), in India it is called *prana*, and in western mysticism it is sometimes called "the universal life force". The deeper your breath the more of this wonderful energy you can draw into yourself.

Breathe deeply: Always breathe through the nostrils rather than the mouth, unless you have nasal congestion. Keep the mouth closed and gradually begin to make the breath longer and longer until you are breathing as deeply as you can without straining yourself in any way. As you breathe in, remember that the deeper your inhalation the more energy you are drawing into yourself. Don't worry about using too much of this energy – it is universal and can never run out. As you breathe out you are cleansing yourself, you are allowing unwanted energy to leave.

Breathe evenly: Try to breathe as evenly as you can – always try to make the in-breath and the out-breath as equal in depth and duration as possible. One way to do this is to do a mental count as you breathe in, and then try to breathe out for the same count, then breathe in again for that same count, etc. It may take you a little while to work out what count is best for you. When you are comfortable with this you can try the following slightly more difficult method of keeping the breath even: instead of counting in your mind count on your fingers. It is tricky at first but soon becomes automatic: you start with the thumb on the tip of the index finger and move it down touching each finger-joint in turn and then up the next finger to the tip and again down the next finger etc. touching each finger-joint. There are four stages on each finger. When you take an in-breath, count the number of finger-joints your thumb touches, and then touch the same number of joints on the out-breath. The advantage of this method is that it leaves the mind free to do more than just count.

0.3 The Complete Breath

Sitting and breathing: Be seated as in 0.1 and start breathing deeply and evenly as in 0.2.

Fill yourself with light: Imagine that the upper part of your body, from the waist right up to the top of the shoulders, is like an empty glass. As you breathe in, visualise that glass filling with a white liquid, or a white light. And as you breathe out visualise the glass emptying. Make sure you really do fill the whole of the "glass" – from just above the hips all the way up to the top of the shoulders. You will find that as you breathe in, your diaphragm will swell out a little, and as you breathe out it will pull in a little. Let that happen. The main thing is that you are charging yourself up with energy, which, in this practice, is visualised as a white light or liquid. It is good to do this for a few minutes to prepare yourself for the other exercises in this workout.

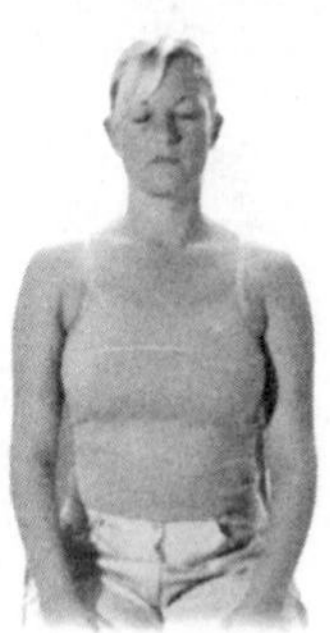

0.4 Watchfulness

Making it easy: Watching the mind can be harder than you might think. In this exercise you are given some hints about how to make it easier.

Visualise a blank screen: Visualise now, in front of you, a big screen, like a cinema screen or a TV screen. If you prefer, you can imagine an empty theatre stage, or if you are artistic, a blank canvas. How you feel is very important to your success in visualisation and meditation, so choose whichever you feel most comfortable with.

Watch: As discussed in the introduction, the way that thoughts enter the brain can be compared to the way that radio waves are picked up by radios. In this exercise, as thoughts enter the brain, try to make them visually manifest on the screen (or whatever you have chosen), and then just watch them. If you are not a visual person, you could try imagining your thoughts being picked up by a radio and then listening to them. You may even find that you can just watch your thoughts without any kind of visualisation.

Detach: With practice you will find that you can watch your thoughts almost as though they were nothing to do with you – you will be able to see them, as it were, from a distance. The ability to "re-tune" the mind in this way can be invaluable in helping you to put things into perspective and gain better control of your emotions.

self
healing
controlling
stress
solving
problems
recharging
your batteries

Keys of Imagination

Science tells us that the brain has two hemispheres, the left and the right, which govern different aspects of the mind. Broadly speaking, the left-hand side of the brain governs the intellectual, deductive, calculating, mathematical aspect and the right-hand side of the brain governs the imaginative, creative, intuitive aspect. Our educational system, and in fact our world as a whole, are very much geared towards training and using the left-hand side. We are forced most of the time to use the deductive, rational aspect of our minds and, for the most part, ignore the creative, intuitive aspect. There is nothing wrong with using the left-hand side of the brain, it's just that we should be using *both* sides of the brain. That is why I make imagination – or *visualisation* – the first key to start to tap into and use.

1.1 Self Healing

It really works! This is not a "miracle-guaranteed" method, but in my own personal experience the vast majority of people who have tried this for themselves have come away feeling better than they did beforehand. Even if there is only a minimal improvement in your physical condition – or none at all – you may find that healing helps you to deal with your health problem from a purely emotional point of view. Having said that, I have come across some truly amazing cases of success with self healing. I remember once I was giving this exercise out on the radio, and a lady phoned the radio station to say that she'd tried it and completely cured herself of an unpleasant condition she'd been suffering from for years. The condition was dystonia, involuntary movement of the limbs, which, by the way, had been caused by the over-prescription of pharmaceutical drugs. She and her doctor were invited to the radio station the next day, and he confirmed that she was completely better, and years later she was still as healthy as could be. One of the reasons why this exercise works so well is that it uses both sides of the brain in balance: the affirmation uses the left-hand side of the brain, the visualisation uses the right-hand side of the brain, and the final part of the exercise uses both the left- and the right-hand sides.

Getting ready: In this exercise you will be using a combination of positive thinking, visualisation, and drawing in the universal life force (see 0.2 for an explanation of the universal life force). Ideally you should be sitting up straight as described in 0.1. The first thing you need to do is to decide what part of you needs healing. As an example, I will refer to "the left leg" in the guidelines below.

Affirmation: Repeat the following affirmation for a couple of minutes: "*My left leg* (or whatever it is) *is getting better and better and better and better*". For this to work, you have to really mean it, it's no use just saying it while your mind drifts off somewhere else. The reason it works is that the *conscious mind*, the part of you which is focusing on the affirmation, is sending a positive message to *the subconscious mind*, which is the part of you which deals with physical functions. When you decide to walk out of a room, it is your subconscious mind which enables you to do so: your conscious mind, the part of you that *wants* to do the walking, sends a message to the subconscious mind, which then activates the appropriate parts of your neuro-nervous system and the act of walking takes place. Your conscious mind couldn't do it alone – it wouldn't have enough knowledge to know which parts of the neuro-nervous system to activate, or how to activate them.

Visualisation: Visualise yourself getting better, and imagine that you *are* better. Imagine yourself doing something that you really love doing but are unable to do because of your poor health. So, going back to the example of the problem with the left leg, you could imagine yourself playing tennis, or running, or jumping for joy or something like that. Really picture the scene. And involve all the senses, not just vision – if you are imagining yourself playing tennis, smell the grass of the tennis court, feel the warmth of the sunshine, etc. Remember the more intense and the more positive the visualisation, the better will be the result. A word of caution: never lie to yourself by telling yourself that you are completely cured; the subconscious mind does not respond well to being told something which it knows isn't true – the key words in this exercise are *imagine*, or *visualise*.

Breathing in the light: On the in-breath visualise white light pouring into you – not just through the nostrils, but through the whole of your being, filling the whole of your body and the whole of the aura around the body. Imagine yourself literally shining – the brighter the better. Then on the out-breath visualise all that light flowing to the part of the body that needs it the most. You really have to put everything into this to make it work, but if you do, you will have some fantastic results. If you are just feeling generally stressed or depleted, then send the light into the solar plexus, situated just above the navel.

1.2 Controlling Stress

Why suffer? Controlling stress, is much more important than many people realise. Suppressing stress can lead to psychosomatic illness, depression, and even reduce your life span. Why suffer when there is a perfectly simple technique you can use to make you that much calmer, wiser and more relaxed?

Identify your stress: One of the great things about "watchfulness" as described in 0.4, is that by watching the mind we can begin to understand why we feel the way we do about any given situation. People often misidentify the causes of their stress or anxiety, or are too afraid to confront them head-on. This not only means that the problem remains unsolved, but can also make the sufferer bad-tempered and difficult to be around – the reason people sometimes lash out over small things is that they haven't dealt with the big thing or things which are at the root of their discontentment. So the first thing to do in this exercise is adopt the sitting position as given in 0.1, and then to become watchful, as in 0.4. As you do this, very, very gently ask your mind to identify the cause of your stress. One way to do this would be to recall a particular low point of your day and ask: "Why did I feel like that?". When you get an answer to this, ask about another occasion: "Why did I feel like that?" or "Why did that happen?" or "What should I have done differently?". Carry on like this, asking, asking, asking until you start to identify the root cause of your stress.

Shine your stress away! When you have identified

the source of your stress, begin to breathe deeply and evenly as in exercise 0.2. As you breathe in visualise a tremendously bright white light pouring into yourself. Fill the whole of your mind and body with this amazing light. Do this for a few seconds then change the visualisation slightly: as you breathe in, *direct* the light *into* the cause of your stress. Thoughts are things – they are real. Visualise the cause of your stress as an actual thing and fill this thing with the white light. Allow the white light to completely overpower your problem, to literally *shine* it away. On the out-breath visualise the thought, picturing it as nothing more than a few fragments of white light, leaving the body. Some people may tell you that you can just breathe your problem out without worrying about filling it with white light first. This may, in the short term at least, help you to feel better, but it will pollute the "mental environment" (or "mind-belt" to use a more technical term). It is highly irresponsible to just throw your negative thoughts out without dealing with them first, as the power of the thought may, to some degree or another, end up affecting someone else.

1.3 Solving Problems

The Open Door Practice: This is one of my favourite practices. It's simple, it's effective and it involves one of my favourite things: *doors*!

Visualise a beautiful door: Visualise yourself standing in front of a door – any kind of door is OK, as long as you like it – it could be a big old castle-door, a beautiful oak-carved door, an ultra-modern looking door – or any other kind of door you can think of.

Ask the question: Imagine that behind this door is the answer to a question you want to know the answer to – the question doesn't have to be a problem in the negative sense of the word, it could be a question about something good. Now, mentally, ask your question.

Visualise the door opening: As you visualise the door slowly opening, imagine white light beaming through it. As it opens wider and wider visualise more and more brilliant white light pouring out of it.

Allow the answer to come to you: As you stand there, bathed in the white light streaming through the door, allow thoughts to come to you. It doesn't matter how absurd these thoughts may appear to be, just let them come to you.

Be patient: An answer might come to you immediately, or it might not. It might pop into your head the next day, or the following week. The important thing about this practice is that you have started the ball rolling, as it were: you have consciously requested information – it may take a little while for the relevant part of your brain to reply. This exercise uses not only the imagination, but also the intuition, which is dealt with more fully in Keys of Intuition.

1.4 Recharging Your Batteries

Why this is so useful: We can become depleted for many different reasons: it might be emotional strain, physical exhaustion, poor health, or just the influence of people around us. Have you ever noticed that some people seem to drain your energy, whereas other people somehow always seem to perk you up? This is all to do with energy – someone's mental, emotional and spiritual "health" (for want of a better word) affects the way energy flows through them, and this energy flow effects everyone around them. Negative emotions like jealousy, greed, hate, selfish anger etc. affect people on a much deeper level than most people probably realise. This practice teaches you how to counteract anything which makes you feel, in one way or another, depleted.

How it works: There are seven major *chakras* (sometimes called "psychic centres", or just "centres"): the base of the spine, the sex centre, the solar plexus, the heart centre (which is in the middle, not on the left), the throat centre, the third eye (also known as the Christ centre) and the crown centre at the top of the head (also known as the Brahma chakra). These are in the aura, which is the psychic counterpart of the physical body – think of it as being like an envelope of energy around us. The solar plexus centre is like a battery: energy can flow into it and charge us up, or out of it and make us feel depleted. In this exercise we use the minor chakras in the palms of our hands to fill our solar plexus with energy.

Positioning the hands: Place the right palm over the solar plexus and the left palm on top of that. The solar plexus is situated just above the navel.

Breathing energy in: As you breathe in visualise white light pouring into the whole of your being, and as you breathe out, allow the white light to flow down both the arms, through the palms and into the solar plexus. You may feel a slight tingling or warmth in the palms as you do this. Carry on with this for as long as you feel comfortable.

The Seven Major Chakras

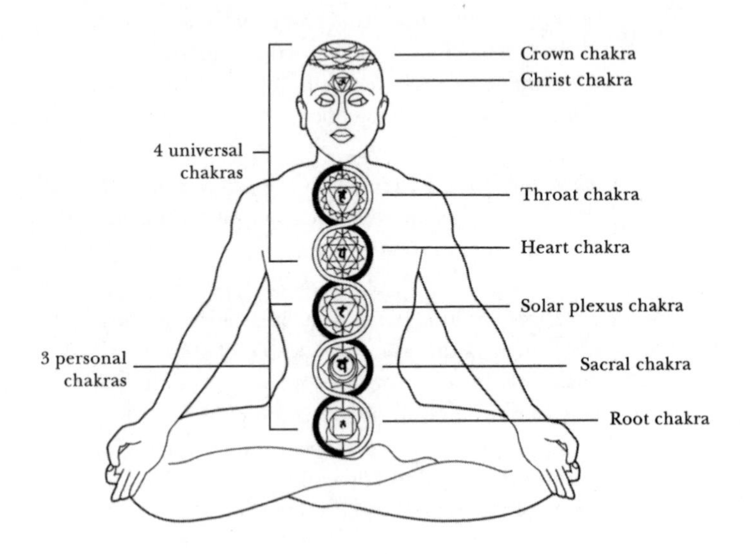

Keys of Intuition

Intuition is a most wonderful aspect of the mind, but, sadly, in the modern world, it is usually vastly underestimated. By using your intuition you are beginning to tap into the superconscious mind, which, though seldom talked about, is in many ways much more important than the conscious or subconscious.

the practice of

Scrying

interpreting

dreams

MEDITATING ON MUSIC

2.1 The Practice of Scrying

What is it? Scrying is a way of tapping into the intuition using the mystical element of water, and is typically associated with looking into the future. Its most famous exponent was probably Nostradamus – but he didn't just scry, he scried in style! He would wear a long purple cloak with stars on it, perform magical rituals and proceed to make mysterious pronouncements about the future of the world. But don't worry: I'm not suggesting that you try to do it like he did it!

What you need: You can just visualise this whole practice in your mind, but, for the beginner especially, the best results are usually brought about by doing it physically. You need a plain-coloured bowl, white is probably best – patterned bowls are not suitable. Fill it with water and put it somewhere flat. Make sure the water is still. You should do this practice somewhere peaceful with a pleasant, preferably spiritual, atmosphere; you may even want to light some lightly-scented incense. Remember: how you feel affects the success of your practice, so always try to make yourself feel as relaxed and tranquil as possible, without getting sleepy!

Get in the mood: Begin to breathe deeply and practice watchfulness as described in 0.4.

Look into the water: Open your eyes and begin to gaze into the bowl. Your aim should be to get completely lost in the water. First of all you will be looking *at* the water *with* your eyes, but you should try to look *into* the water *through* your eyes. The reason for this is to help you to detach from physical vision, to remind you that you are more than this. When you do this your vision may become a little blurred, if it does, don't try to fight it, just carry on. This blurring may manifest as a smoky haze in the water, which might turn into a picture, or provoke a thought in your mind or even cause you to hear a sound psychically.

Detach and analyse: After having done this for a while, try to detach. Now it is time for you to use the left-hand side of the brain to analyse whatever it was that you saw/thought/felt/heard. There are three possible outcomes to this practice: (1) You get no impression at all; (2) The impression you get means nothing to you and you think it's just a result of your imagination wandering; (3) You get a definite impression which really means something to you. If the first couple of times you do this you get (1) or (2), don't worry; nothing has been lost – just keep practising!

2.2 Interpreting Dreams

Types of dreams: Broadly speaking dreams fall into four categories: (1) meaningless rambling dreams; (2) dreams originating from the subconscious mind; (3) superconscious dreams which give us premonitions, inspiration or some other form of intuitively-derived information or experience; (4) out of body experiences (OBEs for short) which aren't really dreams at all. OBEs consist of someone leaving their body and going somewhere and/or meeting someone. I have come across people who, while "asleep", have had proper conversations with deceased relatives, and people who claim to have been somewhere in their "dream" which they have never been to in their ordinary physical bodies but can describe in perfect detail. I have experienced these things myself too. We all dream. Some people say, "I never dream", but it has been well proven that we do in fact all dream now and again – some just find it difficult to remember their dreams. This practice will help you to discriminate between the different types of dreams listed above and guide you into understanding their meaning.

Getting ready: The best time to meditate on your dreams is first thing in the morning as soon as you wake up. Start doing some deep breathing as in 0.2 and begin to practise watchfulness as in 0.4.

Analyse: Go through your dream bit by bit. Try to remember every aspect of it, and make the effort to be as accurate as you can. A word of caution: people often see someone in their dream who, while dreaming, they think is so-and-so, but when they wake up they realise that it didn't actually look like so-and-so. As a general rule, if it didn't look like the person or place you thought it was, then it almost certainly wasn't that person or place – and possibly wasn't even meant to represent that person or place.

Use your intuition: Allow the mind to relax out of "analysis mode" and see what thoughts and feelings come into your mind. Just watch and wait. You will very often find that through this process you can start to tap into your intuition, which was trying to tell you something in the dream. It was only in the dream state that it was able to make you listen – too often in our waking state we shut it out. We are normally far too active, too intellectual, too left-brain orientated: dreaming is an opportunity to allow a higher part of ourselves to speak to us.

2.3 Meditating on Music

Music is an energy: It can inspire us, it can heal us, and it can relax us. The greatness of a piece of music is determined by the quality of the creative inspiration of the person who wrote it and the people who perform it. The greater the piece of music the more inspirational an effect it can have on us, but it is not the greatness of the music alone which determines how the listener will react, it is also the state of mind of the listener. When listening to high-quality music you should always be open to receive the inspiration offered to you. Here are some guidelines for how to achieve this.

Bathe in the sound: Visualise the music as virtually being a "sound bath" in which you are completely submerged. And don't just let the "water" flow around you, let it flow *through* you. Imagine you are outside of your body and watch the music impregnating every aspect of you. Switch off the left-hand brain. Don't try to analyse the music. Don't try to think. Just allow it to affect you. Give yourself to it. When you feel sufficiently absorbed in the music, see what thoughts come to you – not what *you think about* – what *thoughts come to you.* There is a big difference. See what view of life the music is presenting to you.

watch
the music
impregnating every
aspect of you

visualisation
of the
elements
ECSTASY
without drugs
the cosmic
whole
the practice
of the presence

Keys of Inspiration

Some of the most inspired people in history, including outstanding scientists, artists and humanitarians, have received their inspiration in almost instantaneous flashes. It has not come as a result of deduction, or even just feeling good. It is a driving force that virtually penetrated them from outside. We all have this faculty of inspiration. It is a faculty which can change your life and help everyone around you: the more inspired you are, the higher the calibre of your thoughts, and the higher the calibre of your thoughts, the more good you will do for the mind-belt (see 1.2), and the more good you do for the mind belt, the easier it will be for other people to become inspired.

3.1 Visualisation of the Elements

The perfect place: Be seated, breathe deeply and watch the mind as in 0.4. Mentally take yourself to a rural location of your own choosing. This can be wherever you like – it can be somewhere you have actually been to, somewhere that you would like to be, or somewhere idealistic which doesn't physically exist. It can be a mountainside, green fields, a beach – anywhere you like.

The sun represents fire: Imagine that the sun is out,

and that you can feel its warm rays beaming down on your skin, really try to feel it – some people have actually got suntanned doing this, believe it or not! Don't visualise the sun burning you, just visualise it creating a beautiful sensation all over your body. The sun represents the mystical element of fire.

The ground represents earth: You should be standing very firmly on the ground – be it grass, sand, rock or whatever – it doesn't matter, as long as it's natural and firm. Now really try to feel the ground beneath your feet. The ground represents the mystical element of earth.

The breeze represents air: Now feel a little breeze gently blowing against you, ruffling your hair a little as it does so. Feel this cool against your face. The breeze represents the mystical element of air.

The sea/lake/river represents water: Now hear the sound of water. It is essential that there is some water in your chosen location: it might be the sea, or a lake, or a river – it doesn't matter. Kneel down and scoop up a little water in your hands and dab it against your cheeks. Feel the sensation of this on your face. This represents the mystical element of water.

Ether – the fifth element: You are completely alone, there is no one around, but there may be birdsong or other natural sounds. Try to build up the whole atmosphere of the place, not just what you can see but also what you can hear and what you can smell. It has been known throughout the centuries that there are in fact five mystical elements, not four as some people have claimed. The fifth element is ether. This is the element you should now be trying to tune into – it is the atmosphere, the feeling, the energy of the place you are in. Absorb it. Feel it filling your aura and your mind. You can be in the busiest city in the world and this practice will transport you into a completely different kind of energy. When you have absorbed the ether, just become watchful again for a few minutes – see what thoughts pop into your head as a result of having "been to" your favourite place.

3.2 Ecstasy without Drugs

Getting high: You can generate a state of high within yourself without any kind of artificial substance, and the high brought about by this exercise, unlike the high brought about by an artificial substance, will be completely under your own control. This is a very dynamic exercise, and requires a lot of effort, but if you do put that effort in, the results can be outstanding. I have seen people so elated after doing this practice that they have had tears in their eyes. Don't expect much of a result the first time you try this, as it will take you a little while to get used to the mechanics of it.

The bellows breathing: Start breathing deeply and evenly as described in 0.4 but speed it up a bit. Try to make the breath rhythmic, breathing in and out as quickly and as deeply as you can. This practice is called "the bellows breathing" because your inhalations and exhalations should resemble the air going in and out of a bellows. If you get dizzy just stop for a moment and move your head backwards and forwards and from side to side. If everything is going fine then after a few breaths take one large breath and hold it in. Hold for as long as you feel comfortable, then gently let it out in a controlled manner and think back to the happiest moment in your life. Try to recreate the joy you felt at that time, and bathe in it for a few seconds.

The visualisation of the five elements: Do the bellows breathing exactly as described above, but this time, when you breathe out take yourself back to the place you created in 3.1. Feel the place and absorb the ether just as before. Allow it to change you.

A pillar of light: Start again with the rhythmic breathing for a third time, in and out quite vigorously. Keep this going for a bit longer this time, leading up to holding the breath in for as long as you can, just as before. When you have gently let the breath out, visualise yourself in a pillar of white light. Make this a really definite thing, feel it throughout your aura, invigorating you and charging you up with energy. Make the light so bright that if anyone looked at you they would be dazzled. Now stop everything and just watch and see what comes to you. Some people can have a very inspiring experience. If this happens to you then just enjoy it for as long as you can.

3.3 A Meditation on the Cosmic Whole

Oneness: This practice is designed to induce a sense of spiritual peace within you. It introduces the advanced concept of *Oneness.*

The night sky: Visualise the night sky as you would see it in a rural location where there is no light pollution: a purple backdrop covered with beautiful stars. See it stretching on and on and on – limitlessly. Build up in your mind's eye the infinite vastness of space. Try to feel it.

A microbe in the macrocosm: And then come back to yourself, just a small microbe in this massive macrocosm, but an integral part of it. You are a cell in the same whole as all the millions of stars and planets, as all the mighty galaxies. Feel that you are a part of this whole and then start to repeat the two words: "I AM". You are more than your mind, more than even your emotions: "I AM". Say this silently to yourself as you visualise this massive cosmic tapestry of space: "I AM".

A step further: Now you are ready to go on to the next stage, the yoga stage. Repeat the three words: "I AM DIVINE". By repeating this affirmation you are contacting your higher self, your *real* self. Meditate on the true meaning of these words and meditate on the great truth that your own divine self is the same divine self as the cosmic whole.

3.4 The Practice of the Presence

Spirituality: This is an extremely spiritual practice and should always be treated as such. It will benefit you physically, mentally, psychically and spiritually. It was taught to me by Dr George King over thirty years ago, and I have practised it virtually every day since, so I can really recommend it to you.

Hand position: Sit up straight as normal. Place the left palm flat over the solar plexus centre (situated just above the navel), and the right hand on top of it. Spread the fingers of the right hand out a bit to "lock" the left hand in position. Make sure there is no tension in the shoulders. Shut your eyes and try to relax. Note: you should be in the same position as in 1.4, the Recharging practice, except that this time the right hand is on top of the left.

White light: Visualise a white light coming down into the head, charging every cell of the brain, through the neck, shoulders and into the heart centre (or "heart chakra") which is situated in the aura three inches in front of the centre of the breast bone. Some people can see this centre psychically as a lotus flower or a vortex of energy. Charge it up with as much white light as you possibly can.

The Violet Fire: The Mother Earth beneath our feet is, believe it or not, a sacred, living being. In fact She is the most holy entity we will ever touch. With due reverence, gently request that her beautiful violet flame flows through our feet, through the legs, and up into the heart centre. If you have trouble visualising the violet colour, it can be very helpful to look at something violet before you start this practice and then try to remember it. You have now filled the heart centre with the two balancing energies of the white light and the violet fire.

The Golden Sphere: Now combine these two energies and take them upwards through the top of the head, into the Golden Sphere which is just above your physical body. Visualise it as being like a miniature sun – all-powerful in its brilliant golden radiance. This is the spark of Divinity within you. Do not limit your visualisation in any way – really make the most of it. Note: as you take the white light and violet fire as one out through the top of the head, do it gracefully; you should virtually be *offering* this power to the Golden Sphere. Treat this practice as the sacred ritual that it is, and you will get so much more out of it.

The Golden Radiance: Now request from the Golden Sphere that its golden radiance flows down through and around the body and aura, down to the bottom of the feet. Visualise it as being like gentle golden rain, penetrating every aspect of your being. Allow it to *change* you – for the better. Remain like this for a few seconds, then you can say a silent prayer of thankfulness.

Conclusion

Regular meditation will not only affect you while you are practising, but twenty-four hours a day. And the more meditation you do, and the better you do it, the more it will affect you. One of the main purposes of meditation is to re-train the mind – to help you become more intuitive *and* more logical. Imagine a world where everyone meditated – the clarity of vision that meditation offers could virtually bring an end to crime, psychosomatic illness, depression, behavioural disorders, complexes, phobias, violence, war and many other of the problems which plague our world.

Allow meditation to improve your life and it will.

Part II

a discovery of the spirit

~

Since developing the *Meditation – a complete workout for the mind* DVD, CD and cassette with N2K Ltd, it has been tried and tested by thousands of people and the results have been heart-warming; the comments I have received range from: "I've had my first full night of sleep in years" to "Thank you, you saved me". But I have to say that meditation can be more than a workout for the mind – it can take you into your real self, your *Spirit.*

Meditation is an extremely ancient practice which is usually linked with the Indian tradition of self-development called *yoga,* and there are good reasons for this. Arguably, throughout history it has been yoga philosophy which provides the clearest, most systematic and complete explanation of what meditation is and how to do it. However, meditation is in fact a universal practice which crops up in one form or another in virtually every religious and mystical tradition in the world – from Buddhism to Kabbalism, from Sufism to Native American traditions. In fact meditation is so universal that it even goes beyond religion and mysticism – higher states have been experienced by poets such as Wordsworth and Blake, composers such as Rachmaninov, and scientists such as Einstein who purportedly had one of his greatest flashes of inspiration while in a daydream.

When I visited the United States of America in

2002 on a tour to promote spiritual healing, I was surprised to come across a report which showed that there are now 18 million practitioners of yoga in America and that on average each one of them is spending $1500 per year on yoga-related products. This amounts to an estimated total expenditure of $27 billion per year – which means, according to this report, that if the yoga industry were consolidated, the resulting corporation would be larger than Dow Chemicals and only a fraction smaller than Microsoft. This sounds wonderful until you discover that, by and large, yoga has become little more than a series of physical exercises to improve health, fitness and physique. The yoga movement would be so much greater if the physical aspect, which is called *hatha* yoga, were only a part of this explosion of interest which is taking place not only in the United States but throughout the western world. The essence of yoga has far more to do with the mind, and even more to do with the soul and spirit, than it does with the body. Literally, the word "yoga" means "union" – union with your divine self or spirit.

My own guru, Dr George King, entered the highest state of meditation that can be attained on earth, which is known as *samadhi*. He did not regard anything less than this as worthy of the name "meditation". Other teachers have used the word with varying meanings ranging from the most basic definition of simply "watching the mind" all the way through to describing the phenomenon of a meditator being physically immobile and immersed in such an elevated state of consciousness that time itself stands still. This, of course, is much more than just watching the mind; it is complete immersion in a universal state of consciousness.

The definitive source for a complete explanation of the principles of meditation is a series of statements made over 2000 years ago by the great yogi, Sri Patanjali. These have become known as the *Aphorisms* (or *Sutras*) *of Patanjali* and are the basis for numerous commentaries by writers, teachers and gurus through the ages. In all the many traditions of meditation that have been developed since, Patanjali's *Aphorisms* have never been equalled for their all-encompassing analysis of the psychological journey from ordinary consciousness to total enlightenment. In the following pages I have picked some of these aphorisms and attempted to explain them in a modern context. In my research there have been two classic works which I have found invaluable, and would thoroughly recommend to the reader for further study. The first is *Raja Yoga* by Swami Vivekananda, which gives a traditional yogic perspective on the journey to *samadhi* through mental and psychic control. The second is *The Nine Freedoms* by Dr George King, which reveals the new age approach to the subjects of karma and spiritual evolution. I have selected just seven of the 195 aphorisms of Patanjali to provide a glimpse into where meditation can lead us, if, or to be more accurate *when*, we wish to go all the way on this magnificent journey.

Seven Aphorisms of Patanjali

1. *Meditation means not allowing the mind to assume fixed patterns of thought. The meditator is then in his own state. At other times he becomes identified with his thought patterns.*

The basic meaning of this aphorism can be explained by comparing the mind to a lake. Think of a thought entering the mind as being like a stone being thrown into this lake. The fixed pattern is the ripples caused by the entry of the stone (thought) into the water (mind). Through meditation we can learn to still these ripples. This can be achieved by either not allowing any stones to enter the lake, or by having the power to perfectly control the ripple-affect which occurs if we do allow a stone to enter the lake. Watchfulness is the first step in this process: we cannot control something unless we know what it is. By watching the stones entering the lake we gain an understanding of what is going on in our minds, which ultimately leads to the ability to have full control over all our mental faculties. When the waters of the lake are completely still we are in our own state – in that state which is purely what we are, with no external influence whatsoever.

One of the many problems that we encounter in achieving this is that we have all become *attached* to our fixed thought patterns; we are under the delusion that we *are* our thoughts – we regard the "ripples" as integral to the lake, instead of viewing them for what they really are: disturbances in something which is naturally still.

Patanjali suggests that the way to overcome this obstacle is to think of thoughts as "seeds", and to think of meditation as the process of "frying" these seeds. This can be interpreted as follows: as you fry a seed its skin comes off, if you fry it for a bit longer another layer of skin comes off, if you fry it some more a third layer of skin comes off, etc. As you meditate you can remove the outer layer of what a thought appears to be and get closer to what it really is. And every time you think you've got to the real meaning of the thought, meditate again, and "fry off another layer of skin". This process, in its widest application, leads to total enlightenment, or what Patanjali calls, *seedless samadhi* – the point where all the layers of skin have been fried off and all that is left is the Divine Essence present in all things.

All this may sound far too abstract, but, in fact, if you think about it, this philosophy is applicable to all of us every day. The most acute example of a thought pattern we get lost in is any form of addiction. Whether it be gambling, drinking, eating certain types of food or any other behaviour cycle, as soon as we start to believe that we are the prisoner of our desires and habits, we also start to believe that we can do nothing to change them. We can watch and observe these cycles of thought and habitual patterns of behaviour, and in that very process of observation we are able to control them and, if we choose, to eliminate them from our lives.

As with a serious addiction such as drug-addiction or alcoholism, so with every type of behaviour pattern that we wish to change. Meditation empowers us to change ourselves permanently, because in our real state we can determine those thoughts we wish to become detached from. This can seem a little scary at first – people can have a mini identity crisis and think: "What am I if I am not these thoughts and emotions?" But there is no need to panic. After meditation, we return to the world of thought and emotion, to our own predilections and patterns of behaviour. But we return with greater control, greater ability to determine the direction we wish to go in. Meditation brings great freedom because it removes the lie that we are nothing more than a collection of personality traits which we have virtually no control over. We all have the potential to change for the better, and if we change through meditation this change can be a lasting one.

2. *Controlling these thought patterns is achieved through practice and non-attachment.*

Practice refers to continual efforts in meditation to go beyond thought patterns, not to allow them to manifest. The main tool for this is "watching the mind", as explained in Part One. If we can watch the mind, then we must be more than the mind. Most people are prisoners of whatever thought happens to float into the receiver set which is their brain. It has floated in, so they focus on it. It might be a desire, a passion, hunger, thirst, boredom or any other type of thought or emotion. The meditator learns to determine whether this thought will stay within the receiver set or whether they will let it go. That is the great change which meditation brings about. Once we become good at meditating we cease to be the prisoners of our moods. When a meditator wakes up in the morning feeling out of sorts, they can start to choose whether or not to allow that mood to persist.

Non-attachment means not allowing our desires to rule us. This is something that can be practised every day wherever we may be. Just because we want a sandwich, it does not mean that we have to eat one. Just because we want a bigger house, we do not have to buy one. Just because we want to watch television, sleep, have sex, get drunk, work, walk down the street, scratch our faces, phone somebody, we do not *have* to do these things. Our choices need not be made through desire, they can be made from another part of our being, the real part, and in this way we can start to find our "own state" in everyday living. It may well be a good idea to have a sandwich, we may well be hungry and go ahead and eat it, but we are not driven by attachment, desire and the thought patterns and emotions that float into the receiver set called the brain. The meditator who has mastered non-attachment is no longer a leaf floating in the current of a stream at the mercy of the wind and other forces. They are a part of the stream, the current, the wind and the thing which is behind all these forces.

3. *It becomes firmly grounded by long constant efforts with great love.*

Patanjali is very realistic in his approach to meditiation: he makes no rash claim that enlightenment can be achieved overnight – on the contrary he says that meditation requires "constant efforts". To practise once is better than never practising, to practise sometimes is even better, to practise regularly and often is better still, to be ceaseless in practice is best. If you practise regularly you begin to reset your mind – the mind will not have enough time to "unlearn" what you have taught it and slip back into its old ways. This does not mean sitting cross-legged in a cave 24-hours a day for the rest of your life, but that the principles of yoga and meditation can be applied to every aspect of our lives. Yoga discipline is about doing things well, being clear, honest, thorough, and always doing your very best without thought of reward.

If the ultimate aim of meditation is to experience universal oneness, what better way to express this in our daily lives than by recognising everything around us, and within us, as being fundamentally *one*. Actively expressing love for **all** things, through prayer, charity, humanitarian work, fighting for justice etc. is a very potent way to enhance your awareness of the unity of all things. This principle works in two ways: the more you do to help the world, the more aware you become that all is one; the more you become aware that all is one, the more you want to help the world.

Love in its highest form will always contain an element of sacrifice. Doing someone a favour because you want the person you are doing the favour for to like you more is not love – it is merely a strategy to achieve a selfish end. Love, in its higher forms, is totally unselfish. Florence Nightingale is a good example of this: she loved her family as most people love their families, but she loved helping the sick even more – she had a tremendous love for those who really needed her help – so, in the end, despite her family being utterly distraught at the idea, she left England to do the work which she regarded as her duty. By this sacrifice she transformed nursing and, directly and indirectly, has probably helped to reduce the suffering of millions of people in hospitals throughout the world. This is real love. Making a loving sacrifice for those we are not in any way close to is a key to ultimate freedom: it transmutes the limiting thought patterns of selfishness which imprison our minds.

We should also love *ourselves.* There is nothing wrong in loving ourselves as well as others, after all, we are responsible for ourselves. So when we make mistakes, as we all do, a certain amount of patience, tolerance and compassion for ourselves is called for. It comes from the higher part of our being for the lower part of our being – the higher self for the lower self.

"Love" should also include love of spiritual practice. When we meditate we should do it because we *want* to do it – we should do it with joy. A practice session which begins with a negative attitude is unlikely to be very successful. However, only ever doing what we want to do is not good for us either. If you don't want to meditate but you know you should, coax yourself into it: remind yourself of how it can help you, think back to a positive experience you've had with it before, imagine what it would be like if you did enough meditation to become really good at it. Even just *wanting* to *want* to do meditation, if the motive is pure, is a small flower which, with persistence, can ultimately flourish into the mighty bloom of enlightenment.

4. *Friendship, mercy, gladness and indifference being thought of in regard to happiness, unhappiness, good and evil, respectively, control the mind patterns.*

This is a perfect key given to us by Patanjali to control certain types of thought patterns. When we feel happiness we should share it with everyone we encounter. If someone else is happy, we should be happy that they are happy: we should never feel rivalry, resentment or jealousy. Negative emotions such as these will in any case be transmuted by the love which motivates our sense of friendship.

When we are in an unhappy situation, we should feel mercy or compassion, not despondency or bitterness. Unhappiness, strange as it may sound, can be a wonderful thing because it can help us to understand the suffering of others, and consequently motivate us to be more compassionate, and inspire us to actively help people. In this way compassion will transmute any negativity which could, and so often does, creep into an unhappy situation.

When we encounter good news, we feel gladness. If we dwell on this gladness it will empower our minds with optimism and joy. It will train our minds to be positive, which will help us to eliminate negative emotions as and when they arise.

And when an "evil" situation arises we should respond with indifference, thereby immediately pre-empting the anger or vindictiveness which would only compound a negative situation.

These brilliant psychological potions can be applied to virtually every situation we encounter, and will undoubtedly help us to change our daily lives for the better. Patanjali's motivation here is to help us to control our minds and thus prevent thought patterns setting in, manifesting, and repeating over and over again. Psychology has shown us how subconscious thought patterns instilled at childhood can recur and recur until, if they go unchecked, they create illnesses or mental disorders of one kind or another. These can be removed by applying the kind of mind medicine that Patanjali is advocating here. When memories return of life situations, which we think were unfair, or in which we were extremely unhappy, we can apply the correct remedy, such as mercy or indifference, and the situation will be transmuted. It will no longer trouble us and any dependency or illness we may have developed as a result of it, can then be cured. Again, Patanjali gets to the root of the human condition.

5. *[The mind is pacified] by throwing out and restraining the breath.*

Deep breathing, which is featured in Part One, is a brilliant way to bring control over our mental, emotional and psychic thought patterns. Controlling breathing leads to controlling the mind, and even thousands of years before Patanjali delivered his *Aphorisms,* this was regarded as the key to spiritual advancement. By completely controlling the breath through each nostril, being able to hold the breath in or out at will for lengthy periods of time, the yogi can go beyond mind into unsurpassed spiritual realms of experience, in which he or she is bathed in a bliss and a realisation beyond basic mental comprehension. In such a state as this, the yogi can find the answer to any question – not through the process of reasoning, nor even through the process of basic intuition, but through the process of direct perception.

In everyday life practising breathing exercises as often as possible, preferably at least once a day, breathing as deeply as you can, will bring more control and balance to your thinking and emotional behaviour, and will help you to determine your own thought patterns.

All the time, Sri Patanjali is sending out a very strong, positive signal that we can change our lives for the better: we are not the prisoners of our environment or of the personal situations we find ourselves in, even at a deep mental and emotional level. This is so refreshing nowadays when so much general thinking has given way to some psychological, biological and anthropological ideas, which lead us to believe that there is nothing we can do about the way we are. Such defeatist ideas can be dispensed with permanently. We are what we make ourselves.

6. *The meditator who has controlled their mind patterns through concentration makes no distinction between the receiver, receiving and the received, like a crystal.*

This very profound statement gets to the nub of what meditation is really all about. The *receiver* is the mind or brain of the meditator; *receiving* is the mental process that is going on when thought waves are assimilated through the brain; the *received* is the thought itself and all that goes with it. When the meditator concentrates perfectly on whatever they are focused upon, these three aspects all merge into one.

Dr George King divides the journey to the higher states of consciousness into three stages: concentration (fixing the mind on something), contemplation (receiving an intuitive impression from what you have concentrated on) and meditation (being at one with what you are concentrating on). In other words, concentration is absolutely core to all stages of mind-training. It is not a case of suddenly switching out of one stage into another and leaving the first behind. When you are "contemplating" an object, which may include the use of your psychic powers, you will still need concentration to give you the necessary focus. Patanjali views the whole process of meditation as concentration to different degrees of intensity and completeness.

It is interesting that some schools of meditation have frowned upon the psychic powers and mystical abilities which meditative techniques can develop, regarding them as distractions from the main aim, i.e. gaining enlightenment. My own opinion is that it is wrong to make these powers the main goal and purpose of your meditation, but that developing certain psychic abilities along the way can really help us in our spiritual development. Spiritual healing, for example, is a power that everyone can and, I believe, *should* develop and use to help others, and this will itself act as a transmuting agent for certain unwanted thought patterns.

Of the hundreds of psychics I have known and worked with, I have often found that it is the inability to concentrate which has tripped them up. When you gain the ability to "contemplate" it is vital that you maintain this concentrative ability so that you do not lose control over your own psychic abilities and become their prisoner instead of making them your servants to be used to help others. But even correct use of psychic powers is not the end of road: there will come a time when the meditator will reject virtually all psychic abilities and transmute them at an inspirational level into direct perception and knowledge.

Concentration leads to experiencing the state of "being in the now". "Being in the now" doesn't mean never thinking about the past or the future – it means thinking about the past and future *at the right time* and *in the right way,* not allowing the present to be continually clouded by what has happened or what might happen. *Life is what happens when you're busy making other plans* – a statement by John Lennon as profound as some of the great wisdom of the east. There are degrees of being "in the now". To be "in the now" when you are living a fairly selfish existence and not making a big difference to the well-being of others and the world in general, is one thing. To be "in the now" when you have manifested your inner potential, psychically and mentally, and are expressing this in service to others, is a very different thing indeed: paradoxically enough it can take someone of this calibre even more effort to live "in the now" because they will have that much more "spiritual power" which they will need to control in order to bring about the required intensity of concentration.

Some people attain a certain state of peace through meditating and "living in the now" and think that that's all there is to it. They think they've made it, that they are fully enlightened. Gaining enlightenment is a never-ending process: even if you attain the highest state of *samadhi* which it is possible to attain on earth, there is still more to be learnt on other, higher spheres of existence. So one way you can evaluate a "guru" is by applying what I term the "Socrates test": find out if they know how much they don't know, which he regarded as the hallmark of wisdom.

7. *Yama, niyama, asana, pranayama, pratyahara, dharana, dhyana and samadhi are the eight limbs of yoga.*

This is one of the cornerstones of the *Aphorisms* and indeed of *raja* yoga in general. The meaning of each of these stages is as follows:

Yama: non-killing, truthfulness, non-stealing, celibacy and non-receiving.

Some of these are quite straightforward virtues which modern culture embraces, others may surprise. Celibacy, for example, is regarded by some as being not only unappealing but also harmful. And indeed it's true that if it is the result of suppression, then it can cause problems. But as far as Patanjali was concerned, the student who wished to go all the way along this path needed to control all their mental and emotional energies – which would of course necessitate the strict control of sexual urges. Non-receiving is also an unexpected virtue to find on the list, but what it really means is not taking from others more than you give.

Niyama: internal and external purification, contentment, mortification, study and worship of God.

Many of these are qualities you would expect from someone who was seriously taking to the spiritual path. Cleanliness, or "purification", both physically and mentally, is crucial. Contentment is an interesting one to see on the list: it balances mortification, which implies enduring some kind of physical hardship such as fasting. Study of works of great wisdom and divine worship give the student hope, direction, and a greater feeling of love for the Divine in all its various manifestations.

Asana: posture.

In *hatha* yoga there are many different *asanas*, or postures, which have a direct affect on the physical health and well-being of the practitioner. Correct posture is just as important to the yogi as correct diet and the correct amount of physical exercise. Those who use the system of sitting on a hard-backed chair (as described in 0.1 of Part One) will still be able to meditate correctly, as long as the spine is straight, which is the all-important factor. The reason for this is that within the psycho-spiritual nature of all of us there is a mystic force called Kundalini, which will rise through the spine and through each of the major chakras as we start to seriously advance at a spiritual level. It is essential that the Kundalini can rise in natural, unforced fashion when the student is ready for this to happen.

Pranayama: deep-breathing exercises.

This is covered in Part One, but there is a more advanced series of exercises in the book I was honoured to co-author with Dr George King, *Realise Your Inner Potential*.

Pratyahara: restraining and detaching from fixed mind patterns.

This is a stage that people often miss. Pratyahara means preventing the mind from taking fixed patterns of thought and the key to this is the practice of watchfulness or mindfulness, as outlined in exercise 0.4 of Part One. It is an absolutely vital precursor to starting to concentrate effectively.

Dharana: concentration.

This is the cornerstone of success in meditation and personal development generally. You should be able to fix your attention on whatever you determine without distraction for lengthy periods.

Dhyana: often translated as meditation itself.

This is where you move beyond just focusing on the object of your concentration and gain the ability to receive, at a deeper, intuitive level, the energy and essence of that upon which you concentrate. You start to become one with the focus of your concentration and know things about it that no amount of analysis or intellectual deduction can tell you. At this stage you can develop various forms of extra-sensory perception which, according to Patanjali, cause "perseverance of the mind". Far from discouraging these abilities, he regards them as excellent confidence-boosters: they prove to the meditator that they really are making progress. He has a whole section on *siddhis*, mystical powers, which are a part of the journey, but – and this is the crucial point – *not* the destination. Many stop at this stage, they think that they have arrived – they have not.

Samadhi: a deeper contemplative state.

In this state the meditator is in his own space and identified with his real self. At this stage he can know about anything which he chooses to meditate upon. I am not in a position to say too much about this because I have not achieved it myself, so I will leave the last word with someone who has – Dr George King. These excerpts from *The Nine Freedoms* are reproduced with the kind permission of the Directors of The European Headquarters of The Aetherius Society.

Before we can begin to understand meditation, let us consider, first of all, what this state is not. Meditation is not some vague, fluttering flight of concentration, not even a deep psychic state; it is far above all these things. Meditation is only brought about when the all-important power of Kundalini is risen consciously up the spinal column of the aspirant. It rises from the base chakra, penetrates the sex centre and moves higher to the solar plexus. As it is moved upwards, it takes all the power from the sex centre which becomes dormant. It is then moved, consciously, up into the heart centre. As it pierces the heart centre, the solar plexus centre is devoid of its energy and this becomes dormant. At this stage, the meditator becomes paralysed, unable to walk. When the Power is taken from the nerve ganglia which act as a pranic battery in the solar plexus and is risen up to the heart centre, he is no longer able to move his legs and hips. When the power pierces the heart centre, the chakra then blossoms forth and the tremendous power of love can be, for the first time, understood and radiated to all in need. At this stage, the aspirant is capable of advanced psychic vision. He is able to hear the forces within this vortex of power…

If he is then able to raise, consciously, the great power of Kundalini into the throat centre, the heart centre is, by the magnetic attraction of the Kundalini, devoid of energy and the physical heart nearly stops beating. Now the aspirant is sitting absolutely and completely immobile. He or she is in a very deep state of trance. The base, sex, solar plexus and heart centres have had all the power taken from them and they are not operating. The aspirant is unable to move physically, because he is completely paralysed. The blood has almost stopped circulation around the body, because the heartbeats have almost ceased, or in some cases, actually physically stopped. The aspirant is, to all intents and purposes, in a state of conscious death. But the Intuition has not stopped. Inner, shining Light and deep vision are being experienced now. Highly elevated mental energies are now being drawn into the throat centre and the meditator is beginning to understand and appreciate the irrevocable occult laws for the first time. Inside, there is all-vibrant activity.

He can hear the tremendous vortex of power within the Christ Centre above, which physically sounds to him like the rushing waters of a gigantic waterfall. In fact, at first, he cannot hear anything else except this. Then, as he becomes more attuned, he hears the subtle symphony of life. He can hear a tree growing, a man talk to another miles away. He can hear a cloud form 2,000 feet above him if he thinks about it. His hearing becomes so acute that he can hear the subtle sounds of whatever he dwells upon. He can even hear the screeching, high-pitched whine caused by a beam of light as it careers through the envelope of gas molecules which surround the planet. If he meditates upon this supersonic sound, he can become aware of the resonating harmonics, caused as the photons of light are reflected from any object, sounding like a delicately blended symphonic pattern of musical notes which seem, in some strange way, to radiate from all sources at once, yet echo and re-echo as though passing on through some gigantic tunnel.

He can transfer his hearing above the atmospheric belt and hear the strange almost elongated sounds of full, vital space. He becomes a Master of all things audible. He can hear a million notes, most of which he could not name. He could write, if he were consciously able to move that is, great symphonies of nature's wonderful sounds. He would speak, if he were capable of moving his lips, greater words than Shakespeare ever wrote.

The aspirant is now an Adept.

If he can now, consciously, raise the Power of Kundalini together with the forces of the throat centre even higher so that the Christ Centre fully opens, he becomes a Master for that time and he is capable of meditation for 5 minutes, 10 minutes, 50 years, 200 years, it does not matter. His body becomes completely immobile, almost cold. His breathing is barely perceptible. The only heat in the body is a thin band of warmth around the top of the forehead which stops rigor mortis from setting in and this warmth is just enough to keep the blood in a state of semi-suspension…

The Adept then becomes one with that upon which he meditates. When he consciously reverses this flow of Kundalini until it is back down at the base of the spine again, therefore allowing him to use the physical body as he did before, he comes out of this state as a wise and enlightened person.

In this excerpt, Dr King parts company with the traditional use of the word, "meditation", by defining it exclusively as a very deep state of *samadhi*. Few people have attained this elevated condition in the history of humanity. It is wonderful to know, though, that there are those men and women who *have* done so, and it is a goal for each and every one of us to aspire towards.

Conclusion

The journey of a thousand miles, as the Chinese sage Lao Zi stated 2,500 years ago, begins with a single step. Your single step might be to start practising the meditation workout in Part One. If, at a later stage, you wish to go deeper into it, there is a wealth of knowledge available through yoga masters such as Sri Patanjali, Swami Vivekananda, Dr George King and many others. There are other traditions of meditation too. But whatever you decide to do, please remember one thing: this path will only work if it is focused round service to others. There was a time when the yogi could drop out of the world and concentrate purely on their own development and gain complete success if they applied enough effort to it. But that time has now passed. In this, the Aquarian age, we *are* our brother's keeper. The world is far too fraught with crises for us to be able to ignore our obligations to others. In fact, the most worthwhile, lasting motive for personal development is, and always was, to put you in a better position to help others more: to have greater wisdom and healing power so that you can use this in service.

We are taught by all the masters that the greatest realisation that we can achieve in meditation is the realisation of the oneness of all life. There is no sense therefore in trying to be an island by concentrating purely on your own development to the exclusion of others. Advance yourself so that you can serve the whole more effectively; this very act of service will in turn help you to advance; and so the positive cycle of success will continue. This will be a true, lasting discovery of the Spirit – the same Spirit which exists within all life.

Appendix

For further information on lectures and workshops relating to meditation please contact:

The Inner Potential Centre
36 Kelvedon Road
London SW6 5BW
Tel: 020 7736 4187
Website: www.innerpotential.org
Email: info@innerpotential.org

Personal instruction for groups or individuals based on Part One of this book is given by life coach Tony Perrott, who can be contacted at: tony@alternativelifecoach.com.

The DVD, CD and cassette, on which Part One of this book is based, are published by N2K Ltd, The Studios, 8 Hornton Place, Kensington, London W8 4LZ.

For further information on Mind Body Spirit Direct Ltd, leading UK multimedia resource centre for those seeking the inner life, contact:

Inspirations for an empowered lifestyle
755 Fulham Road
London SW6 5UU
Tel: 020 7731 2828

Website: www.mindbodyspiritdirect.co.uk
E-mail: info@mindbodyspiritdirect.co.uk

notes

The following pages are to enable you to take notes detailing meditation experiences and thoughts.

Refer to them often and observe the changes that meditation practice brings to your well being.

Date: Time:

notes

Date: Time:

notes

Date: Time:

notes

Date: Time:

notes

Date: Time:

notes

Date: Time:

notes

Date: Time:

notes

Date: Time:

notes

Date: Time:

notes

Date: Time:

notes

Date: Time:

notes

Date: Time:

notes

Date: Time:

notes